MY EXPERIENCES
WHILE OUT
OF MY BODY

CORA L. V. RICHMOND

Cora Lodencia Veronica Richmond (April 21, 1840 – January 3, 1923) was one of the best-known mediums of the Spiritualism movement of the last half of the 19th century. Most of her work was done as a trance lecturer, though she also wrote some books whose composition was attributed to spirit guides rather than her own personality.

For more information about out of body experience
and to view other books in this collection visit www.astral-institute.com

DEDICATION

Primarily

To My Heavenly Guides:
Those Teachers and Inspirers who, in early childhood, awakened and have unfolded the Spiritual gifts that were mine, and have borne forward to the present hour the work appointed me to do; and
To Those Beloved Friends
who, having received the ministration through my humble instrumentality have constantly given from hearts and hands the sympathy and aid needed to perform that work - and during the feebleness of the body have sent strength and succor; and especially to the beloved and loving friends: Dr. Chas. H. BUSHNELL, whose skill, healing power and faithful attendance were given without stint or measure and most lovingly, Sarah J. ASHTON, co-worker for more than a quarter of a century, Assistant Pastor of my Congregation and, above all else, faithful, devoted friend, without whose unfailing care and constant helpfulness for long months my spirit could not have returned to its human habitation to take up its assigned work, This imperfect record of experiences is most lovingly and gratefully inscribed.

Cora L. V. Richmond.

THE RELEASE

It was true then: I was suddenly and finally released from my body; "this time," I said, or thought: "I will not have to return."

Many times, almost numberless, I had experienced the wonderful consciousness of being absent from my human form, of mingling with arisen friends in their higher state of existence, but, until this time I had always known that it was only for a brief season and that there was a tie - a vital and psychic tie - binding me to return to my earth form. But norv; now; could it be true? Was I set free to live and work with the Beloved - the dear ones - in this their higher, more perfect state?

The Best Beloved, those who had preceded me into this wondrous life, came thronging around, by degrees, to welcome me: not all at once, but first those who were by tenderest ties the nearest and the dearest.

They did not answer my question: "Have I really come to stay"?

The Guide - the Guardian, took me gently in charge that I might not even think of the form I had so lately left. A great sense of relief; of being set free from the limitations of the body, filled me, far greater than I had ever experienced before. A feeling pervaded me that all of me was released. It surely seemed that my work in the human body was done: that the last word was spoken, the last pen-stroke made.

O, the wonder, the unspeakable joy of thus being united with the Beloved - those whom I knew had never died, but had thrown off their garments of dust for the more beautiful raiment of the spirit!

In a narrative written for others to read one cannot dwell minutely on the sacred meetings with those who were ever nearest and dearest; those of the household, related by ties of consanguinity and those who were kindred in spirit, united to one in thought and aspiration. All that such reunion means, more than can be dreamed or imagined where one is in the human state, was now my possession.

"Turn away, turn away from all thought of the Earth-form;" said the one appointed to lead and guide me in this newer, grander flight. One by one - or in groups - the dear ones of the Earth-home joined us, welcoming me ever, yet ever evading the oft recurring question, "Am I really here to stay?"

My attention was continually attracted to some group or company that had not been seen by me— always a surprise to find them "all there." They would smile and seem to answer, "Yes, all here," in our own particular states, and doing our own appointed work."

THE VASTNESS OF THE SPIRIT REALM

There was a perception of great Light, a consciousness of Illumination, an awakening to the vastness, the unlimitation of this Realm of Spirit.

O how often, when in "dreams" or "visions" I had been permitted and aided by my Guides to visit the Spirit States, this inner and higher Realm, I had longed to remain! But ever willing to answer the call of duty, of added work to be performed by me, I would return to fill my place at the appointed time. Now; Now?

All else was swallowed up- eclipsed by the wonderful experiences that came - the Beloved Presences - the vistas of luminous Spirits! This was a state of Super-Consciousness; the awakening of faculties and perceptions before unknown, of being aware, almost without limitation: of KNOWING.

Whatever is the nature and state of the real Ego this seemed as near to the Absolute as one could well conceive! There was so much of me! There was so little of me! There were so many and such surpassing Spirits! How one shrinks in the presence of the mighty ones ! How one expands in the Knowledge of the Infinite: His Image!

Often in approaching a transcendent Light there would appear an atmosphere of ensphering tints - there would also seem to be a sphere of sound, of surpassing music. On being admitted to that sphere it would prove to be a group of spirits who thus in accord are Light and Harmony. Where one can enter such an "atmosphere" communing with such a group it is because one has need of and is in harmony with the spirits of that group.

SENSES MERGED IN PERCEPTION

Objective scenes seemed ever to be adaptations to my state, and would often vanish as I became aware of the minds or spirits suggested by the scenes.

"All human sensations, as sight and hearing, are readily perceived by one awakening to spiritual states to be but manifestations of consciousness through the physical limitations to which the spirit in its mental states of earth becomes accustomed. But here all is merged in perception - where one perceives and understands," thus said the Guide.

This added consciousness - uniting or releasing the faculties - is not all at once: I found myself thinking in the accustomed channels, in words as well as thoughts, listening for replies instead of knowing that the answer had been thought to me, really was there before I had questioned; of looking for beautiful forms and scenes instead of perceiving the Soul of Beauty which was (is) everywhere.

I became more and more aware that the whole of me, released from the fetters of the bodily senses, could perceive and receive more perfectly the answer to every question, even before its formulation in thought.

"Formulation is a process of limitation, sometimes of hindrance," said the Guide. "A feeble comparison of what 'perception* really is may be found in an artist (of Earth) whose prepared mind (and therefore vision) sees the beauty in a landscape, a sunset sky that another sees not at all, or dimly. Prepared senses are the result of prepared minds, of being pervaded by the awareness of the Spirit," said the Presence.

It is of little avail, however, to attempt to bring into outward forms of thought and expression the perceptions one is aware of while one is in that inner state, excepting that they relate to conditions under which those loved and loving ones in that state can reach and change for the better the sorrowing hearts in human life, the shadowed conditions of earth existence.

THE BODY IN CHARGE OF GUARDIANS

After a time (I did not know it as time) I became aware of being led to where the earthly form was still breathing, being cared for and imbued with breath by a beloved Guardian spirit and by devoted friends in human life. I was to return after all ! It was necessary to keep my spirit en rapport with the body as the Psychic Cord was not severed that connected body and spirit. But not at once was I to return.

These periods of calling my attention to and visiting the body were brief - just enough to keep the "vital spark" alive, and aid the dear attendants in both worlds to prevent the complete separation which for many days seemed imminent.

A VAST CONGREGATION

It is well known to those who may be interested in reading these pages that during all the years of my mortal life (since the age of eleven) I have been brought before audiences and assemblies of people - many thousands; among them were hundreds who became friends - some of them life-long, some of later years. I had known of the "passing on" of very many who had been members of those audiences and of my own "Flock," but I was not prepared for the vast congregation that came out of their respective groups composing a still greater concourse to meet me, nor was I prepared to realize that I knew most of them as friends on Earth!

There were those who had heard the utterances of my Guides through my lips when I was a child; those who had attended and were my personal friends when I was "still in my 'teens"; and those who in later years had been of the audiences in many places; and those of my own beloved Congregation!

How difficult to realize that they were all gathered into the larger "Congregation of the skies." Each and all unfolding, working in whatever line of knowledge and work was theirs to attain and achieve! And to find all the treasured jewels of friendship more bright in the added lustre of the larger life; the flowers in the Garden of true Affection growing more and more transcendently fair!

This is indeed Heaven! Next in blessedness to the Homes of the Best Beloved which are the very Kingdom of Heaven!

MINISTRATIONS OF SPIRITS

It was wonderful to note the ministrations of spirits to those in other less fortunate states - especially to those in Earthly forms. Wherever the ties of consanguinity were also of real affection the spirit guardians of the household responded to the "call," perhaps only a thought, a longing, or a silent prayer for aid and strength, or a need unknown to the one ministered unto.

Time is not a factor on the spirit side, the response to a need - an aspiration, a prayer is instantaneous. Where there seems to be delay, and often doubt in the minds of those on Earth as to the presence and ministration of the loved one who has been summoned, it is because of Earthly barriers, because those in the human state cannot perceive - and many, alas, are not willing to receive the spirit friend. I saw that the usual barriers are: Uncontrolled, selfish grief - mourning for the one who has "passed on" and often forgetting the other dear ones of the household who are left ; seeking for the communion to forward a purely selfish purpose; and, in general, the obstruction of false education, theological and material, through which the spiritual faculties have been closed for generations.

When human hands and hearts, even though the latter is wrung by pain, seek to help others who are in sorrow or need, then the way is opened and the helpers are helped by the ministering ones.

To mourn the friend as utterly "gone" who has only dropped the outer garments of the dust is to close, for the time, the avenue of communication or ministration. Long must the spirit helpers work and wait for people to be ready to receive their response to the call for aid. So many did I see who could not reach the recognition of their loved ones that I wished over and over again that there were more real "Message bearers" more to give comfort to those that mourn! And then the Presence answered: "Not all are ready to whom the Messages now are given, nor are those protected adequately who are the chosen Instruments for Message bearing, but the seed is being sown and will take root in thousands of lives.'

THOUGHT-FORMS

I was shown those who existed in the thoughtforms and scenes of their recent human states: Such as these were surrounded with the "things" (forms of things) familiar to them on Earth, and apparently necessary to their happiness even in the new state of existence. These scenes illustrated that our lives even in the human state, consist largely of "states of mind" that we see the things we are accustomed to see, or have trained our minds or wishes to see omitting many and sometimes most of the things of beauty and of import that we might see.

The spirit-states that are "exactly like the scenes of Earth" are composed of the thought forms of the spirits' imaging or reproduction, and are the reality to them. I recalled the weaving of a web that I had once seen an industrious spider perfect and he was afterward caught in his own web. I wondered if we are not often in human life - and the states that immediately follow the weavers of many such "cobwebs"? These thought-webs seemed to proceed from the minds of the spirits fashioning them and in which the spirits seemed to be ensphered, sometimes enshadowed. Before my questionings had taken form in my mind the answer came from the Presence: "No, they are not enmeshed by the thought- f orms ; their creation is the result of the present condition; remove the power to produce thought- forms, i.e., to create ones ow T n environment and you remove all activity of mind. As the Spirit unfolds the thought-forms change and then disappear as perception takes the place of limitation by the senses."

With the almost axiomatic proposition that "our world of life is what we make it" our spirit-surroundings and conditions the result of our states of unfoldment, it became less difficult even when returning to the limitations of human organism to understand the conditions of existence in the "next stage" of personal experience beyond the "transition" misnamed "death."

Spirit states are as varied as are the personal states of those composing them; the knowledge - or lack of it - possessed by the person IS the spirit state, i.e., knowledge of spiritual principles.

Oh, if one could coin new words, or new understandings, in order better to express that which one knows when set free from Earthly environment! Yes, the New Understanding; that is the great need; and that must really be attained by unfoldment, jgrowth from within, the pervading all illuminating power of the spirit.

Those in the spirit states who were reproducing the familiar scenes of their recent Earth conditions were satisfied and even very happy - especially when the scenes so reproduced were of a nature that had brought comparative happiness in Earth life - in their ability to make things seem "exactly as they did in Earth life," not even knowing that this similitude was the result of their own thought-forms instead of being inherent or organic in the "spirit land."

Interesting and absorbing as were these lessons of observing, the process of weaving their thoughts into the forms most desired or needed by the spirits producing them, there were many whose reproductions were of the shadowed kind and were not voluntary, but results of the deep impress that the shadows of Earth-experiences had made upon their minds. No one illustration could serve - but all states and conditions that I could realize were shown.

TIME NOT A FACTOR

Time does not seem to be a factor in the realm of spirits except as related to people and events in the human state with which spirits have connection. It was, however, a source of continual wonder and surprise to note the changing forms and atmospheres in the surroundings of those with whom I was brought in contact. I saw spirits who, when in Earth-life had been in positions of external power - usually considered "exalted" - as of kings or rulers —the result of no "merit" or achievement of their own, but the "incident" or "accident" of birth, who were arrayed in their ovjn thought-rohes of power, but closer observation would reveal the poverty and meagerness of their "Robes of Royalty" and they were sometimes seeking somewhat with which to clothe themselves, something to conceal their paucity of raiment and surroundings. Most of those, however, who had held such positions as are the result of "titles," "rank" and "castes," seemed endowed with perception enough to know that those external conditions are not perpetuated in spirit states, unless one has become so imbued with the idea that "titles," "wealth," and outward "honors" are valuable in themselves. And that the "Divine Right of Kings" is indeed a "right" derived from Heaven.

THE TRULY GREAT ARE HUMBLE

I saw many of those who had been poor in worldly possessions, even despised and scorned among men or put to death because of their advocacy of an unpopular "cause" now radiant in their own spiritual brightness, unconsciously

"Wearing their sunbright thoughts For Robes of Royalty."

Ah! How beautiful were they! These of the shining faces and radiant hearts! Ever intent on trying to aid humanity, whether in shadowed spirit states or in Earthly conditions.

One may not give the names (even if one knew them) by which these in the various spirit states were known on Earth. I saw many who were known to be Great: Great in thoughts, deeds and words for the enlightenment of their fellow-beings. Ever were they humble, as ever are the truly Great. None in spirit life are outwardly adorned with the "honors" given to them or their "memory" by a tardy World. The truly exalted are far too intent on ameliorating the adverse conditions of spirit and human states to take note of the praise and pomp of Earthly "celebrations" in "memory" of them, sometimes tardily bestowed.

To be truly Beloved by an individual, a country or a world is indeed blessed, and exalted souls do know and understand the true meaning of being "appreciated and beloved."

The Light of the Shining ones, the Great ones, is not dimmed in the brightness of the higher spheres, for they are of its light a part.

SPIRIT GROUPS AND INSPIRERS

It is because of the spirit possessions that those of kindred thoughts, perceptions, aspiraitons are attracted to each other and form groups - not conventional or arbitrary - interchanging ideas - purposes - and working together for others. I saw them "moving upon' the minds of those in Earthforms whom they could reach, sometimes singly, sometimes in groups, as the conditions might require. The Student in his library, the Inventor in his "work shop" or laboratory, the "Discoverer" in his Observatory searching for new worlds or on ships of "exploration" sailing for Unknown lands, more particularly those who are seeking to solve the vexed "problems" of human life.

Ah! It was indeed a scene of wonder to see each and every spirit thus intent on doing good to his kind, imparting some needed thought, some "clue" or "thread" of an intricate proposition that would solve the whole! Long are these "Inventions" and "discoveries" known in Spirit states before the one is "born" into human life that can give them outward Expression. How luminous seemed the Atmospheres of Spirit thus surrounding those in Earth life when the Heavenly presences were near! And such lives are always luminous in their own brightness or the Higher ones could not "draw near" and inspire them.

The people know the names of some of those now on Earth whose "discoveries," "inventions," and works have transformed the world! Those arisen ones who aid in bearing forward the Works Beautiful, direct their thoughts to such as are ready in Earth life. Here are the "Thinkers," whose knowledge of the Truths of the Universe constitutes the source of all power, Ideas that born of those Truths reach the minds prepared to receive them and move the world. We saw and paused among assemblies, groups pursuing their usual course of conferring, interchanging of ideals and preparing to impart more and more the knowledge that is theirs - as minds are prepared to receive.

Knowledge is imparted by adaptation.

All such imparting of knowledge must be by adaptation. The Spirit is attracted— would be from the very nature of the Spirit - to the one best prepared to receive from that Spirit. Thus the subtle law of imparting knowledge by adaptation governs the realm of spirit and constitutes the basis of deciding concerning "Guides," "Guardian Spirits," and all "ministering ones." Affection determines the intimate personal guardians.

FROM SPIRIT TO SPIRIT

It was most interesting and enlightening to see - as I was permitted to witness - a number of who are in human states receiving from luminous and illuminating spirits some new application of science or art, some new presentation of Truth! The minds of Earth so impressed are not narrowly questioning "from whence do the ideas come"? Fearful, if from another mind that those receiving them may "lose their Individuality"

Such minds know that Truths belong to minds - and that somewhere are greater minds than one's own - who can impart knowledge. *Truth is the common heritage of souls*; of Intelligence; and happy is the mind, spirit or Angel that can perceive or receive it from any source. Intelligence alone perceives and imparts Intelligence.

The process of imparting knowledge from spirit to spirit (whether those imparting and receiving are in spirit states or still in Earth forms), grows ever more and more interesting as one passes into greater awakening and perception of the realities, the verities of spirit. "Teaching," "Education" (in the human sense) only exists in those states or conditions in the spirit realm where the human methods and forms of thought still govern the minds of the spirits.

Love is the great Illuminator in all realms and worlds, and thus adaptation of Teacher and the one to be taught must be the keynote to all reception of knowledge.

One would like to say so much while comparing the "Educational" process of spirit states with the methods of Earth (excellent as some of the latter have become); but one must hasten to record added experiences while they are near to the outward consciousness from within. For when one enters again into the daily life of Earth, even although it is ever pervaded by those surpassing scenes, the vividness of the higher state becomes dimmed by the necessary veiling that human conditions bring.

THERE IS AN ANSWER
FOR EVERY QUESTION

Everything that I wished to know found ready answer; even before the wish was formed into thought. I could realize that the answer came from the Guide, who was my teacher by adaptation. I could realize that for every real aspiration there is ever an answer; in fact that the answer from within and above prompts the aspiration, the wish to know. That there is a solution for every so-called "problem"; for, in the final analysis, there are no "problems" - *except states of non-perception.*

All this and a thousand times more of inward awakening came to me as I grew in the perception of the Knowledge of the Spirit.

THOSE WHO LOVE
THEIR FELLOW-BEINGS

I saw a countless multitude growing brighter, more resplendant, as I was led nearer. Among them were those more radiant than the others - greater, it seemed, in the scope and power of their spirits.

I recognized - not always from personal knowledge on Earth - some of the individuals who were there, centers of groups of radiant ones, those who, when in Earth life "loved their fellowmen"; and who, by word and deed had sought to overcome the errors and abuses heaped upon humanity. Their battles with tongue and pen (no armaments or weapons of war), their shining armors of Righteousness - were finally known and appreciated by many minds (souls) on Earth.

One whom I had known from early childhood came toward me with the group of his friends and relatives, whom I had also known. He greeted me as he was ever wont to do when we both were in Earth forms. Though advanced in years before he left the form, he was ever youthful, ever calm and peaceful; yet firm and forceful in his advocacy of his convictions of Human Brotherhood, and the final triumph of the spirit over errors of human conditions in Time and Sense. By those who knew his life and works he was considered a "leading and inspiring mind" ; to many he was a Prophet of the "Good time Coming." How my spirit thrilled with this meeting with him and his household and the group of friends who were with him. One question I had often asked in mind, or had wished to know concerning it:

Had he - this friend with whom I was then conversing, met in spirit states the one who in a distant land of Earth had said: "…is the greatest man America ever possessed"?

The one who said this to a prominent writer was also a "lover of his fellow men," but the two had never met in Earth life. The question was not asked; before it could be formulated the answer came: "Yes, we have met and often confer together. In all essentials relating to the Supreme Realities of life and the growth of human beings toward perfection through knowledge of Divine Truth and Love we are in perfect accord." I then perceived from among that goodly company the one approaching of whom we had been speaking; our thought of him and our appreciation had attracted him to us. Long and earnestly they spoke of the things to be when the children of Earth shall be set free from the shadows caused by ignorance. I more and more perceived some of the personalities of those illuminated ones, and more than once was I surprised that those who had been of such widely different conditions, environment, education, habits of mind, and, one would think, opposite spiritual states could be together!

The Presence aware that the surprise would exist, said:

"As you already know, differences of birth, nationality, outward rank and even of education, are not real differences in spirit. These are (and were) all lovers of their kind - lovers of Peace through Enlightenment and Righteousness, and they are now, as they were when on Earth constantly seeking through interchange of high Ideals, to find the best means for helping others - to lift the clouds of ignorance from the minds of earth; even now one is within your vision whose presence here will surprise you." I saw a stately form and recognized the one who, as the head of a great Ecclesiastical organization had in the "Prayer for Peace" issued a short time before he had passed from his Earthform.

MAY THEY (THE NATIONS) REMOVE THE CAUSES OF WAR.

As a lover of humanity, a promoter of Peace, he seemed to stand near these shining ones, many of whom when on earth (and now) have never recognized any Ecclesiastical Authority. Of course, I knew that all such lines, barriers, and human standards are removed - or rapidly vanish - in spirit states among Enlightened minds. And that they realize, as this one must have realized, that the Earthly "Office" and all its outward symbols and adornments cannot continue in a realm where the real nature stands revealed - the nature of the spirit.

All these composing this radiant assemblage were intent on reaching and for their good, acting upon the minds of those on Earth for the "Promotion of Peace on Earth and Love to All."

Alas and alas! "Those engaged in actual war - the war raging between one-half the nations of the Earth that call themselves 'enlightened' cannot be reached until the leaders and rulers have learned the lesson taught by bitter experience." So the Presence said, and so I had perceived, saddened by the thoughts of the awful human suffering that must ensue.

THE SHADOWS OF THE CONFLICT

Then I was shown the dense Shadow - the awful darkness that seemed an engulfing abyss : the scenes of the conflict now raging on Earth. That which I saw (then just begun), seemed, however, more to represent the spiritual and mental states of Rulers and Leaders than the physical scenes of battles. I saw the bright spots where the ministrants of mercy were rallying, regardless of nationality or "class," to aid those physically wounded, to breathe a word of comfort to those injured mortally who were "passing on."

Above the terrible scenes of battles I saw those in the "rank and file" of the armies and navies who were so suddenly wrenched from their bodies. Their first thoughts (as their last thoughts had been), were of those loved ones from whom they were suddenly parted when ordered "to the front." They were aided to find the dear ones (alas where were the "homes"? now desolate. Many of the families scattered and in deepest suffering, great physical want, and greater grief.)

They tried, often without avail, to comfort and aid the dear ones, their own states of mind and grief over the separation preventing them from effectively ministering to their loved ones. They soon became aware that the aid could not be material, that spiritual strength and consolation must be from spiritual sources and that they might, if themselves strong in spirit, move upon the minds of others in human life to aid those dear to them.

It was a wonderful sight to behold the ministering spirits succoring, comforting, instructing those thus suddenly thrust into spirit states ; none but those endowed with the Divine Gift of loving compassion - like a Florence Nightingale or a Clara Barton - could so successfully aid those spirits thus ruthlessly torn from their human ties and forms. It is an awful sight! Yet the spirit "Rescuers" are there! The "Red Cross" of the skies finds its way to those who need the help and guidance.

In a measure the Soldiers, all who must go to war on land or sea, are better prepared for the sudden change than those hurled into spirit life by "accident" of shipwreck or other disaster, or by volcanic or earthquake shock. The Soldier knows that he is to confront possible and even probable physical death - and being thus prepared often is less surprised and shocked when he finds himself "out of his body." Yet, wherever the need may be, the "strong helpers" are there: above every scene of human sacrifice, whether Cataclysmic, "natural causes" or the result of human ignorance and neglect, or the self-seeking aggression of war, there are they - the dear ones, the strong ones, the saving ones!

All cannot be aided to at once perceive the newfound condition : everything must depend on the degree of spiritual preparedness, which is often greater among the humble and lowly - who have a line of simple life, simple love, simple duty to follow than among the more complex mental and moral states of the "leaders." The real state, spiritually, determines the "condition" of the spirit in spirit life.

Nor were the "clouded" and "shadowed" scenes of Earth life found alone above the lines of battle. There were sometimes deeper shadows among the scenes of "pleasure" and "mirth," mocking splendor of wealth and its opposite of want, squalor, misery, the toll of human sacrifice is not always in the "death" of the body. There are vortices more terrible than the volcano's fiery breath or earthquake's yawning mouth; the palace often seemed more densely shadowed than the hovel; while the dwelling, though a cottage, brightened with Love shone out like a star of splendor.

"Spiritual knowledge, the unfoldment of the highest from within, this alone can change the "shadowed states" of Earth into brightness. Every life must be reached; every mind touched and awakened by the spirit; the "good" that is within each must be brought forth."

TURNING FOR RESPITE

From the storm-scenes of contending forces, from the darkness of Spiritual night, from the uncertain states, like dim twilight, one ever turns in spirit to the Beloved, to the groups of loved and loving ones that constitute the "Home of the Spirit." "Spiritual rest is change," respite from witnessing the un happy conditions, the shadows of spiritual states that one cannot at once remedy. "Rest" is not idleness: communion, companionship, "Working together for those who can be aided - this is rest. The "Home Group" ever intent upon ministering wherever and whenever needed, afforded the respite sought. Such memories of Earth-experiences as had been kept alive in the sacred altar-flame of true affection and home ties; such interchange of Ideals and experiences as the later years had brought; such knowledge of the blending of the spirit and the mortal states, the guardianship and ministration of the loved arisen ones over those in Earth- forms, this was rest. Blessed respite ; blessed communion; one would never be ready, it would seem, to part with such companionship.

Nor do we ever "part" with the truly loved. Whatever duties we must perform for those in spirit or human states, those most in accord, those nearest and dearest are ever with us "whether in or out of the body."

Our human phrases, and even our usual thoughts seem superficial, weak and puerile when endeavoring to describe the divine realities of the Spirit. We never "part"; we can never be "absent" from the Beloved. Yet the shadows of human existence: "time and sense," and outward "change" and "circumstances" are upon those who make "the house of clay" the limit of their mental and spiritual possessions.

REUNION WITH LOVERS OF "PEACE"

Returning again and often to the bright sphere composed of "those who love their fellow-beings"; from among them came those whom I had known - with whom I had, as a humble worker labored for some cause - this time a few, especially two or three last seen in Earth life at the Hague Peace Conference (1907). "Ah, how well we then knew - as well as even now when the conflict rages - that the nations (44 in number) were not all, indeed but few of them, seeking for 'peace* ; the permanent establishment of a Court of Arbitration for the world! Each was there to 'test' the others; nearly all endeavoring to gain some concession from the others to aid in their own selfish future aggressions"! Such was the thought flashed from my friend of the brilliant mind and noble heart who came with others to greet me. And the dear lady who took me in her arms and kissed me when we parted there at the Hague even as she did now, said: "We meet again, and here there is sweet Peace - but O, the horrors of the war! And you, you will return to Earth for further work" She gave me her blessing with such love as her grand soul can give.

The other one, he of the brilliant mind and facile pen, he of the awakened and illumined spirit, said: "Yes, you will return to Earth for added work (even after those many, many years of work already performed) , we will aid you, we all must aid those who are working to enlighten the minds, to awaken the spirits of those immured in the materialism of Earth. How dense we all are until awakened ! Sorrow smites us, then the fountains of the Soul come forth; our spiritual Guardians can help us then, and we begin to know. That was my case on Earth. Now I realize how little I did know, but I am grateful that I was not an entire stranger to this realm of spirits, and there is all eternity in which to grow in knowledge."

MESSAGES FROM FRIENDS

From those whom I met in their homes of peace and love and work were many messages to be delivered in person by me to the dear ones on Earth - messages that might be of interest here to show that true affection and personal watchfulness are more manifested from the spirit side of life than people know; even those accustomed to spirit communion and ministration do not realize all that they might of this nearness. These messages are too intimate and sacred, however, to be given here, and they breathe all the fervor of the *real life and love of the Spirit*. I shall communicate them to those to whom they were sent.

THE SPIRIT-HOME OF THE CHILDREN

But O, the Children! the Children! What can one write or say? What words adapted to tongue or pen can convey an adequate idea of the spheres in which my spirit has often met those darlings of both worlds? My own baby girl, who passed on many, many years ago and who has grown to womanhood in her spirit state, has ever been my constant companion, as a guardian spirit, during my busy hours of Earth life, as a pilot and gentle helper when through sleep or trance-control my spirit was set free to join her and visit the realm of the children.

These "little ones" are often wiser in knowledge of the spirit than mortals of more mature years.

Blessings ever attend the presence of a babe in the home of love on Earth and, in the highest sense, doubly blessed are those who having possessed such a treasure know that if the babe passes from mortal sight the treasure is still theirs, a babe - growing among the flowers of the gardens of spiritual life is as

"A light within a light,
A joy ensphered in joy."

Such a child becomes a sacred guardian unto the household.

It was indeed an enchanted realm into which we now entered. Although visited many times during many years it now seemed more real, more beautiful, more perfect.

As far as vision (perception) could reach - as vast as the mind could compass or conceive there were children, children everywhere! Sporting in the light of their own brightness and joy; they were embodied sunbeams, weaving rainbow tinted thoughts into forms of beauty; flowers, flowers everywhere; songs of birds and child voices mingling with murmuring waters amid scenes of rarest beauty. Ah, the spirit realm of childhood; the playgrounds of the skies!

Not only children, but those of larger growth, parents, teachers, friends were there to teach, to aid, and to grow in greater knowledge and usefulness. Sometimes the children are the teachers to those older in Earth years.

Isles of light, radiant with flowers and verdure and surrounded by iridescent waters! Could one ever picture the thought- forms of these lovely ones?

"Let us make rainbows," exclaimed one fairylike child among a group of playmates, some of whom were new in that realm. A questioning look came into the eyes of those addressed: "How can we make rainbows?" A child-teacher drew near and said: "I will show you; come with me."

The five or six eagerly responded.

"Take hold of hands," the Teacher said, "and have no fear, there can be no rainbows without clouds and light."

I was permitted to follow, with sight or ken, as the Teacher led them away, away from those enchanting scenes to where the clouds and shadows hung dark beneath and around them.

They had drawn near a large city of Earth. "O let's not go here," said one, "it seems so dark." But the others urged her on.

Soon one little boy among them said, "See, there is a little girl. She is cold and is crying on the street; she is hungry too, let us help her." They drew near, and the child, feeling comforted (she knew not why), sobbed more softly and prayed:

"O, my mamma in heaven, can you hear me and send help to brother and baby - you loved us so?" Then the spirit children saw a man approaching; they fairly pushed him toward the weeping child to whom he spoke kindly asking:

"What is the matter my little girl?"

"O, sir, my mother is dead, and my brother is sick and the baby has nothing to eat. We're so cold in that room."

"Can you take me there?" asked the man, and he held out his hand for her to lead him. She clasped two of his fingers with her tiny hand and led him through the dark streets to a narrow alley and up some dark, creaking stairs. Yes, there was little brother crying for "mamma," for "sister," and the baby asleep but sobbing.

The kind-hearted man saw everything at a glance.

"Don't cry, my little man. I'll be back in a few minutes. Take care of them, little lady, until I come."

The spirit children had helped, and helped ; they saw the spirit mother looking very sad, bending above the baby, and then above "little brother." They also tried to comfort him and help the little girl. They saw the man go to a telephone and talk with some one and they could see and feel the light of kindness with which he spoke and in which the answers came. How quick he was! He found a place to buy food. He came back soon, built a fire, warmed some milk, gave the other children something to ease the worst pangs of hunger. Presently a woman came - such a kind heart! She too worked fast. She gave the baby some food prepared in the milk, helped the little sick boy, who was more in need of bodily comfort than anything else, soothed and fed the little girl who, little mother that she was, at once aided in caring for the baby. How the spirit children worked too! They had made the man see and hear the little girl, had aided in guiding her to the dismal room called "home", had helped him find the telephone and the place to buy the food, had helped the woman to find the place, had helped take care of the children and comfort them and the spirit mother.

"Now," said the Teacher, "we will return to our beautiful home."

One little boy whispered to the Teacher: "I know there are more children and people who need help down there. Can we go again and help?" "Whenever you choose to make rainbows or flowers or other beautiful things we will go." And they rejoiced.

Lo! As they passed through the encompassing clouds circles of rainbows o'er-spanned them and paths of rainbows guided them to their spirit home. When the other children saw them approaching they sang, "O, the rainbows! O, the rainbows!

When you dry the tears of sorrow and help those in need you make rainbows." All spirit children are taught to visit the scenes of Earth life. The home and its loved ones, where they are missed, ever attracts them and they are taught to minister, to aid, to guard. If they had no home on Earth they try to aid those who still remain in the "orphan" realm of human life. while out of my body

THERE ARE NO ORPHANS
IN THE SPIRIT REALM

Mothers whose babes are in the Earth life help to care for those "little waifs" thrust out of human existence - and for spirit children that pine for Mother love.

Children whose parents are in Earth life are taught to aid and comfort those in the home as well as those who have no home. Especially cared for are the little "waifs" who were not welcome in the Earth-forms - even those who have not seen the light of earthly day - not always from among the poor of earth were they driven, especially those abandoned by the unfortunate or misguided mothers. These and all are "mothered" by the spirits whose hearts are filled with mother love. And here it is well to note that not all who are earthly parents are real fathers and mothers, and many who are childless - work night and day in the "asylums" on earth to save some neglected, forsaken, child. These are real parents.

What greater "punishment" could there be than when the human mother has turned away from the sacred gift of motherhood, she meets, on entering spirit life, her own neglected babe who welcomes her there? "Coals of fire!"

It is not always to visit scenes of sorrow and want that the spirit children are led to the earth : Houses, schools, playgrounds, "Lyceums" where the little ones of earth are taught, places of entertainment and amusement where they play, and sing, and grow; there also are the playmates of the spirit home mingling with them and endeavoring to impress them with thoughts and deeds of loving kindness with things of beauty.

Returning to the Realm of Spirit Children one finds such respite from care, such constant sources of happiness, such fashioning of forms of beauty. Oh, that all could know! Knowledge of all this has reached but few on Earth ; yet more and more will human minds be pervaded by the methods of the Skies.

Those who have given new methods of "Education" to the people of Earth have been inspired somewhat by these Teachers in spirit states. Froebel, whose "Kindergarden" system was intended for "children" of all ages; A. J. Davis, whose "Progressive Lyceum" system was not intended exclusively for Sunday training of children but in its inception was a reproduction of the "teaching" in spirit states (as far as his mind and inspiration could reproduce such beautiful methods.) Even if one could give in human language the form of teaching (or methods) of the spirit states, the law of adaptation prevailing in the higher realms might not always be available in human life.

How beautiful to know that growth - and the best opportunity for the highest unfoldment with most loving teachers and Guardians surround the darlings who have passed from the households of Earth.

Here then, O human parents, O sisters and brothers, you who miss the bodily presence of the one who occupied the "vacant chair," you who feel the pervading sense of the absence of the loved children: here they are; bringing to your very homes and hearts, could you but realize it, the love, the knowledge, the wisdom, the beauty of the skies.

BEAUTY AND HARMONY

Ever from childhood through all the years of Earth-life beautiful scenery, tints of earth and sky, music, in fact all beautiful sights and sounds, strongly appealed to me. In the spirit states I noted that harmonious colors, beautiful scenes, and often exquisite music greeted me as we approached groups of radiant atmospheres, encircling spheres of light; such exquisite sounds of harmony as one dreams must be the "Music of the Spheres." On approaching nearer I would perceive that the tints and sounds, as they reached me, were the radiations of thought, the spirit activities of these thus ensphered who have attained real harmony. They were not MAKING beautiful colors and music, but LIVING them.

THE "ARTISTS"

Perhaps I have elsewhere written that music in spirit states does not always accompany the one who was a "musician" on Earth; and harmony of color, beautiful surroundings may ensphere one who never thought of being an "artist." Their lives have been interwoven with sweet and loving thoughts and deeds.

That which would have been a source of surprise had I not previously known it was that "artists," "painters," "sculptors," "musicians," and even some of the "poets," known by those names on Earth, are not fashioning landscapes, portraits, or carving from stone the images of lovely forms, nor are they fashioning or weaving into music or verse some classical or other theme: All of those who were "geniuses," all who were Idealists, true lovers of their £iW, find here (in spirit life) their highest happiness in ministering to others, in moving upon the minds, hearts, spirits of those to whom they are adapted, until they perceive the Soul of Beauty and fashion it into their lives. The "Masters" of art: painters, sculptors, builders, construct their temples and adorn them with lives - the true images of beauty in thought, feeling, aspiration, achievement.

Music is perfect Harmony, of one life with itself and others, of many lives in all their highest purposes. Such are the creators of the "Symphonies of the Skies." Those who had "Talent," hoping to achieve the works of "Genius" - sometime, somewhere, are still intent on fashioning reproductions or imitations of natural objects and scenes, or impressing art students of Earth to produce such effects. But these are not the creators - every "creation" is from within and must live" said my Teacher.

One wishes for a magic pen, or for a perfect Gift of Expression, to convey in language the subtle consciousness of the Beauty and Harmony that meet one as one is led to the "Atmospheres".

"CREATORS OF BEAUTY."

More wonderful than all else was the knowledge that many who had never painted, carved, builded, or traced the "score" of musical composition were surrounded and pervaded by such ineffable loveliness that one could weep for very joy on perceiving it.

"Art is Great, but the perception of the Soul of Beauty is Life! Love!" said the Guide.

One perceives in such states as were there revealed that the true "artist" has not always been known among his fellow human beings, moving upon the world of thought, influencing other lives by the beauty and harmony of their own natures, these seem, when viewed from the spirit, to constitute the real artists.

"Is not the Temple of the Soul a Living Temple, is not the art of molding the mind to perform the mandates of the spirit more to be sought for and greater when attained?

"Eternal in the Heavens" are the Temples "not made with hands," so said the Guide and so I perceived more and more clearly.

In marked contrast to the foregoing were the thought-forms surrounding some of those who had been "artists" on Earth: broken lines, inharmonious colors, discords, sharp and jagged corners - all portraying disturbed conditions of the unruly thoughts and impulses that had possessed them in Earth-life.

I had interesting glimpses of those who were "*working with themselves.*" One who was considered "eminent" in art on Earth was cutting, carving, breathing upon *an image of himself.*

"What is he doing?" I exclaimed, now really surprised.

"Removing the angularities and errors of his own nature: jealousy of other artists, the deepest scar; selfish love of human praise - that overweening desire for adulation; unwillingness to accord to others appreciation of their true merits," replied the Guide.

Later, I saw that artist self-renovated, and one whom he had envied derided and scorned, when both were in Earth life, working together, producing, through artist minds on earth, works that possess the merits of both with the added tone of harmony; the strength of one being merged in perfect accord with the grace and loveliness of the other, blending in wondrous works of Beauty.

This was a wonderful lesson, serving to illustrate that at first, and possibly for some time after entering spirit life one's chief occupation is - or should be - removing one's own limitations; but this can not begin until one is aware that one has the imperfections; to be conscious of one's faults is half the remedy.

Bodily imperfections, infirmities and disease, unless retained psychologically by having constantly encroached upon the mind, or deformities that are dwelt upon mentally, are dropped with the body; but such infirmities of mind as are born of an undue "egotism," undue self love, (the capital "I" around which the universe revolves), must be removed before the spirit can enter upon real "work- As with artists so with those eminent in science or any department of human thought and endeavor ; the truly Great are ever the most humble ; realizing that however much they know, and however clearly they can think "the universe is full of things we do not know"; as one of the great ones aptly said.

I had met one - a brilliant mind - who in Earth life was gifted in many ways, chiefly mathematics. He had breakfasted on billions, dined on duodecillions, supped on sepdecillions, he wrote to the rythm of "logarithms," and worshiped at the shrine of the calculus! I tried to imagine what he might be doing. Perhaps he was measuring the immeasurable or calculating the uncalculable ! I saw him! Where was his Observatory? Where his maps, charts, instruments? The answer swept over and through me with a great thrill.

"The knowledge that comes to the spirit is instantaneous - if one is ready - how can one use even the most perfect instrumentalities and methods when time and space are eliminated? Truth is perceived: in homely phrase "No ladder for the air men," "no mathematics for the soul!" I never could have imagined how quickly he would "perceive." He had attained the real knowledge of wisdom and love.

The poet-prophets of the world, those who have sung in immortal verse the Truths of the Skies: Truths of Freedom, Justice, Love, Spiritual Exaltation, moved by the theme of their songs, using their art as a setting to the Jewel of Truth, these endowed ones knew that without the inspiring theme, the words, the rythm would be empty bubbles, glittering nothings.

ALL ARE TEACHERS

All exalted lives (spiritually) moving and living in similar planes of thought - born of their spiritual states - are attracted to each other in spirit life for the interchange of perceptions of Truth and bearing forward the work of illuminating such minds on Earth as are ready to receive along the lines of human progress and unfoldment, imparting "the things they are ready to know."

Spirits, the wise ones, do not make the mistake, as many do in human life, of trying to force upon the minds of those whom they teach the truths or knowledge for which those minds are not prepared:

"Arithmetic first, after that geometry and higher mathematics," is the rule in Earth schools. So in the instruction by spirit Teachers there is adaptation to the pupil not only of the Teacher but of that which is to be taught. There are "ministering spirits" adapted to every condition.

I could but marvel at the wonderful workings of these principles that govern the influence of "mind upon mind" - really spirit upon spirit; so much more complex yet more potent than the "forces" and operation of the "laws" of the material universe - "laws" so little understood, "forces" so dimly perceived.

"Most of the people on the Earth-plane know so little even concerning the things and forces most intimately connected with their bodily existence: the sunshine, the air they breathe, the earth beneath them, the sea, and the heavens of Stars; we must not wonder over-much that they know little or nothing of this inner, though more real, realm of Spirit."

This was from the Guide. Anticipating the question that was welling up from the mind: "Why do not those on Earth know more of these spirit states, more of their own conditions spiritually?" The answer had already been given, and as we passed on the Teacher said:

"Growth, unfoldment, waiting, working."

CO-WORKERS

Among the groups and assemblages whom I met and with whom I was most frequently in communication during this surpassing sojourn were the arisen co-workers in the "Movement" with which my lifework has been most identified:

"SPIRITUALISM"

In the work of a life-time as a chosen "instrument" to bear "glad tidings," to promote the knowledge of spirit existence here and beyond the change called death, and the ministration from and communion with the arisen ones, I had met in outward existence every leading mind and every worker (medium) known in the Spiritualistic movement.

We were always friends, always co-workers, sisters and brothers bearing forward a great Truth. Very frequently during this wonderful visit in the realm of spirit I saw them - either alone or in smaller or larger groups, renewing the companionship that had been so beautiful and delightful when we had worked side by side in human forms.

In your memory, dear reader, or in your reading scan the list of names who were first known as "Investigators" then as "Spiritualists," and the names of those known as MEDIUMS (there were no "Psychics" in those days.) I knew and loved them all. I met them all. Each one in spirit life is still engaged in imparting this knowledge - most important of all that human beings can receive - concerning Spiritual Truth. Existence, life, love, work beyond the change called death;

SPIRITUALISM AS A MOVEMENT

I had ever been instructed by my Guides, was given to the world when needed, and when there were those upon the Earth who were ready, when the "ages were ripe" for its coming.

In spirit states of Earth and in the realms far beyond were those who knew the "day and hour" had come for "moving upon the minds of Earth with this new illumination."

There was from the "smallest" to the "greatest," from the seemingly "least" to the "most important" of the manifestations a concerted action. The "rappings" at Hydesville were no "accident," the visions of Clairvoyant and seer, the writings and trance utterances (phenomenal) were all a part of this Stupendous Movement. All, all, under guidance of those wise Spirits who knew what the people of the world needed and gave it to them according to their needs.

Necessarily many extremists and "imitators" would be attracted to the subject - like driftwood following or borne upon every new current of thought - but it is safe to say that Spiritualism during the sixty-seven years since the "Rochester Knockings" has attracted the attention of more eminent minds in every department of human research (and convinced them too) and given knowledge and consolation to a greater number of people than any movement or system of knowledge in ancient or modern times. With those who are willing and anxious to be classed as Spiritualists it is knowledge of life beyond death - and of the presence and ministration of the beloved arisen ones.

So spoke my Guide to me and to the group of co-workers who had come forward to meet and greet me. How young and beautiful they were. Always I had noted in earth life how beautiful the dear ones are when one has been for a time absent from them - and here, in this realm of perpetual youth, with the freedom from human pain and cares that some of them had so bravely borne, I could but note the beauty that is theirs.

In the interchange of thought and experiences with these arisen co-workers I could readily understand that being brought into direct personal relationship with their "Guides," "Inspirers," "Teachers/*" "helpers" and with each other, they had become more and more aware of the true meaning and nature of the gifts (mediumship) that were theirs when in the form, and they realized that even those "Inspirers" and "Teachers" were also the instruments of higher and wiser Spirits.

One sister worker said to me "I always wanted to see my Guides, as you did, but I could not, for the gift of spirit vision was not mine. Now I understand what it means to 'see with the eyes of the Spirit' and I am satisfied."

Those who had been my most intimate co-workers had many things to tell me of their "awakening" into added perception of spiritual things and of the work assigned them in their new state of existence; still ministering, still trying to lift the veil, mostly of ignorance, that divides mortals from their arisen ones. Many were the loving messages sent to friends and loved Companions still in Earth life. "Tell them you sarv me here in spirit life, and I am ever near them, in response to a thought, or wish or especially a need, guiding, guarding, aiding."

It seems better to receive a message from one who has "been there," who has actually seen and conversed with one's friends "face to face" and "spirit to spirit." So, in the treasure house of my spirit are stored those messages to be given whenever I meet any of those loved ones in human life to whom I was so fortunate as to bear a message. It is to them alone that the message for them can be given.

The transcendant brightness and spiritual beauty of that assemblage of spirits - from guardian spirits of relatives and friends to the wisest and most advanced that one could see, are beyond my power of language to express.

There is no formal taking of one's "place" or "position" no ceremonious "assigning" of "duty" or "work," but in groups and larger companies, as well as in personal ministrations, a mutual understanding of purpose, according to adaptation. If a united or concerted action upon earth-minds for any given purpose is needed it is readily perceived and entered upon by all who are in accord, and is performed by such methods as enlightened spirits readily understand.

Human minds are better prepared to comprehend the methods of spirit communicating with spirit since "wireless telegraphy" and other recent scientific wonders have been achieved, not that the process is similar in any degree, but being prepared for the new revealments in science also prepares impartial minds to know of the more subtle powers of the spirit. "Volition" in its highest analysis is the one attribute of the spirit by which other spirits know - through perception, what is being imparted, but there must ever be accord, sympathy, adaptation.

From some of those who had been my friends in my early life and who were "leading minds" in this cause, and in other subjects of human interest, I received many thoughts and suggestions concerning the present status of the "movement" (Spiritualism) and what they now think of the possible and desirable results of "united action," - "organization" for the work and the workers. These and many other themes must be left for opportunity, time and strength to reveal, as my work goes on in human life.

One notes the same minds and spirits in many assemblages of the different branches of all purposes for aiding humanity. Even as when on earth the "Pioneers" in "Anti-slavery," "Equal Suffrage," "Temperance," were the same staunch body of men and women, ready now as then to respond to the call to give a voice to Truth. In the assemblies for promoting "peace" by "those who love their fellowmen," there was the universal sentiment: "Peace must be born of Justice and Justice can only come by true Fraternity."

"My country is the world;
My countrymen all mankind."

This is the standard extending to include "All Souls."

"It seems to inhere in the very nature of human life that men will fight for: (1) Personal liberty: freedom from physical bondage and involuntary servitude; (2) For defence of those nearest and dearest enshrined in the "home"; (3) For country when it represents the "home" and those "Ideals" to which the heart ever clings."

To "remove the Causes of War" all selfish seeking, all aggression by any nation upon the rights of others must cease, "and this must come by growth, by enlightenment in the cardinal principles of justice, love and truth." These and many other thoughts were given forth in that assembly.

A great wave of uprising among the women of all nations was predicted in favor of conditions that would "make for peace" leading to united efforts between the most enlightened men and women of all nations to the establishment of "Peace born of Right - Not Might." The Peace foretold by poets and sages of all time. Yet all agree in that wonderful assemblage, that "treaties of Peace" are without avail unless the moral force of the nations - among their leaders, rulers and a majority of their people - is sufficient to dominate; and make just treaties binding.

As individuals are now expected to adjust their difference in Courts of Law (often misnamed justice), and it is the aim of a majority of citizens not to encroach upon the real rights of others, so the time must come when nations will agree to a similar method in adjusting possible differences that may arise; and this much can come even before the real millenium of "Peace on Earth and Love to all Mankind." There must be some other International Tribunal than the battlefield! Earth, sea, and air, must not be held in bondage for physical carnage!

In the final "Day of Peace" even Peace Tribunals will not be needed, but now - "may Angels speed the Day of Peace born of Justice." In most instances I could tell the personality, or human name, of each one giving forth a particular thought, and all were in accord. Alas, I could also perceive that they saw, in viewing the conditions of Earth that "the end is not yet."

I cannot mar this wonderful visit - this respite from pain and cares of Earth by dwelling too long among the shadows, warclouds and darkened states of Earth life. As beyond the storm clouds of Earth's nearest material atmosphere the sun always shines glorious and with resplendent brightness, so beyond the horrors of war the desolation and ravagement of nations incident thereto, beyond the storms, earthquakes, and cataclysmic throes of nature, the Sun of Spiritual Hope and Love ever shines surpassing fair, and all the Angelic and Spiritual Hosts are ready to aid, strengthen, succor the spirits enshrouded in time and earth conditions.

THE RETURN

More and more frequent were the summons and the visits to my mortal body, to reimbue, as it was now found possible, with my spirit, to restore with the personal presence, the body within which the vital spark had been kept alive by blessed Guardian Spirits and devoted friends on Earth.

More and more the spirit "Home friends/' the Best Beloved, and the Guides encouraged the thought of my return to fulfill the appointed work on Earth. I had prayed to be allowed to remain, to let the body pass; but now, gradually it is true, the idea of resuming the human habiliments, the garb of the material body, became less repugnant, and I finally freely said: "Yes, I will go as that is the appointed way."

Have you, dear friend, who may be reading these imperfect fragments of a perfect experience, (as any narrative must be) ever visited some fair garden, some sequestered home of dearest friends, a place radiant with beauty and enchantment; where there were flowers massed in rarest combinations of color and fragrance, fountains murmuring in answer to the summer winds, music, such as seemed a part of the enrapturing scene; have you enjoyed this with the chosen friends that alone could make the scene sacred, the Best Beloved? And have you known the reluctance to return to the "outer world" of daily routine of care, perhaps of pain? Ah, then you know in the smallest degree what it meant to me to return to my bodily form!

Yet even now the soul of all that was mine in that wonderful, surpassing state is ever with me; nor will it again be absent from me - since it is enfolded in my very being. I am more complete now, even in the body which ever divides us from the Soul of Life. "You will be with us again and often," they said; the Guide said no formal "farewells," no "leavetaking," but everywhere from every Dear and Blessed one "Blessings, Peace, Joy, and Love go with you into added Strength and Work."

And here I am : ready to help the body to grow stronger, and to willingly, joyfully, in the future as in the past, perform the work assigned me - until - they - call - me - Home.

AN ADDED WORD OR TWO

The possibility of the spirit "leaving the body" for a time and then returning and resuming its usual activities has been demonstrated many times. In some instances the temporary separation was caused by accident, illness, states of coma induced by anesthetics, trance, either of spirit control or hypnosis, and sometimes a voluntary absence or activity not suspending the vital functions of the body. It is also undoubtedly true that during sleep - especially that restful, dreamless sleep that betokens a normal state of mind and body, the spirit avails itself of the opportunity of restoration by spiritual methods and activities not possible while urging the body to do its bidding. Not only Spiritualists, Psychologists and Psychic Research students have well authenticated cases of the undoubted activity of the Spirit apart from the body, but many prominent physicians have recorded their experiences with patients whose bodily functions were suspended, even to seeming dissolution, and upon the unexpected resuscitation of the subject there would be a vivid account of active experiences in spirit - usually pleasant scenes and meetings with friends long passed into spirit life. These visits to "heaven** would be sometimes tinged with the religious bias of the subject, but this is not strange in view of the fact that spirit states are conditions of the mind and spirit experiencing them.

Among the most familiar popular illustrations are those narrated by Elizabeth Stuart Phelps, especially by "Gail Hamilton" who, being thought "dead*' returned to her body, narrated to her pastor the experiences she had during that period of suspended animation and resumed her pen, remaining in mortal life a considerable time thereafter.

Although not usual, this class of experiences is not so unusual as many imagine or assert. And the writer having been from childhood accustomed to the "other state" (Inner, higher), of consciousness can distinctly trace her experiences in that inner realm as forming fully a third if not onehalf of her life-experiences.

The "realm of spirit*' in which she has so often found herself a participant is, therefore, no unfamiliar realm; in fact if called upon to decide which state is the reality - the life, she would unhesitatingly say : the inner state, the super-mundane realm. Of the many eminent men of Science in both Europe and America who have come to a knowledge of the truths of Spirit existence, continuance of life after transition, - and the writer has known them all personally, except the one she is about to mention, - probably Sir Oliver Lodge has approached the subject of "psychic Research" (Spiritualism) with a mind the best prepared to receive (perceive) Spiritual Truth. I say this with the utmost reverence and admiration for the long list of names - eminent alike in their personal qualities and scientific attainments, whose lives have been made brighter by a knowledge of demonstrated future existence and a belief in the Immortality of the Soul. Shall I name some of them? Hare, Mapes, Denton, Wallace, Crookes, Varley, Zollner, Flammarion - the list is almost endless.

Sir Oliver Lodge has not only recently, and very publicly, announced his full belief (knowledge) of continued personal existence beyond the change called death, but the possibility of communion with those "gone before" and the certainty that he had personal evidence beyond cavil or doubt, proofs indubitable, of the presence of and communication with his particular friends, but - and this is the point I wish to emphasize - in his earlier utterances on this subject he said in effect: "When I become aware that the human spirit while still animating the body, or not released by death, has such surpassing powers, 'telepathy,' Voluntary action' apart from the body, showing conclusively that the activities of the mind are not dependent upon the physical organism - I concluded there must be evidence to show that the spirit can and does survive the body." This and much more was in his published statements concerning his investigations in connection with Psychic Research - showing that he approached the subject not only from the "effect to cause" line of usual scientific investigation, but had already in his quickened perception the vivification of a-priori knowledge leading from "cause to effect"

One would like to accumulate and set down in condensed manner all the available evidences of "absence from the body" - of which the writer has a large and increasing store, but this writing is more distinctly in the form of a message for this particular time.

With our own "other world" within and about us, moving "like wings of light on dark and stormy air," with such unused, wonderful powers, what wonder that one having partaken of the bounties of that inner realm longs to awaken the "sleeping" spirits of those in human life - or, more correctly speaking, tear aside the veil and show

how wonderful are the dormant powers within each person: Soul-powers more active, perhaps, than any are aware! Who can tell, until the film of mental blindness is removed, how great may be the works accomplished by the spirit when the body sleeps, when one is "absent minded," or when thinking intently of a particular friend, one finds at that very day and hour the friend had "passed away"? It is of the "Substance that dreams are made" that we shall ultimately find our divinest realities, our verp lives are fashioned

This narrative of "experiences while out of my body" is only a prelude to those vaster heights, those more inner scenes, that I hope sometime to be able to record: The Symphony is Life itself whose theme of Love is Endless, Endless, Endless.

The Author.

Made in the USA
Monee, IL
21 May 2022

96652152R00028